RAINCOAST POCKET GUIDES

Plants of the
WEST COAST TRAIL

COLLIN VARNER

RAINCOAST BOOKS
Vancouver

Edited by Scott Steedman and Simone Doust
Designed by Ingrid Paulson

Raincoast Books
9050 Shaughnessy Street
Vancouver, British Columbia
Canada   V6P 6E5
www.raincoast.com

Raincoast Books acknowledges the ongoing financial support of the
Government of Canada through The Canada Council for the Arts and
the Book Publishing Industry Development Program (BPIDP); and the
Government of British Columbia through the BC Arts Council.

NATIONAL LIBRARY OF CANADA CATALOGUING IN PUBLICATION DATA

Varner, Collin.
  Plants of the West Coast Trail

  Includes bibliographical references and index.
  ISBN 1-55192-481-1

  1. Botany—British Columbia—West Coast Trail. I. Title.
QK203.B7V37 2002   581.9711'2   C2001-911682-9

Printed and bound in Hong Kong, China by Book Art Inc., Toronto

1 2 3 4 5 6 7 8 9 10

TABLE OF CONTENTS

The west coast of Vancouver Island is one of the world's greatest natural areas, and the West Coast Trail is the doorway to this enchanted land.

The history of the West Coast Trail dates back to 1890 when a single strand of telegraph wire was needled between the trees from the lighthouse at Cape Beale to Victoria. At that time, the area was known as the "Graveyard of the Pacific." Heavy fog, hurricane-force winds and a rocky shoreline spelled doom for many ships. It wasn't until 1906, when the passenger ship *Valencia* crashed into the rocks and 126 of its passengers died, that the federal government upgraded the antiquated telegraph line into a life-saving trail. These days, more than 8,000 people hike the trail each year.

Mild winters, long summers and high rainfalls have made the West Coast Trail into a truly unique temperate rainforest. The vegetation is so thick and lush that the area can boast the greatest weight of living matter per hectare in the world, as well as some of the world's tallest trees.

The trail ascends and descends through three main vegetative areas: the rugged shoreline; forests, both first-

Red paintbrush

and second- growth; and elevated bogs. The growing conditions and plant life in each area differ enormously. Harsh winds

Dwarf western hemlock in the elevated bog between Cullite Creek and Walbran Creek

and saltspray keep the coastline coifed with windswept Sitka spruce, red paintbrush, yellow monkey-flowers, red columbines and dune grass. Yet only thirty metres inland from the crashing waves is profound quiet. Here the spruce, cedar and hemlock reach gigantic proportions, the sword and deer ferns form tropical groves and the salmonberry, thimbleberry and blueberry bushes are draped in fruit. The elevated bogs between Walbran Creek and Cullite Creek are a horticulturist's playground. Cleverly installed boardwalks dissecting the bogs allow for close observation without harming the fragile ecosystem. Insect-eating sundews carpet the floor, and deer cabbage and bunchberry bubble up and over the boardwalks. Ageless hemlocks and pines form miniature open forests reminiscent of giant bonsai gardens. Labrador tea, bog laurel, gentians, cotton grass and skunk cabbage add to this concert of nature.

This guide describes the vast majority of plants to be encountered along the trail. Each species has a fact sheet with three or four entries. DESCRIPTION presents the plant and how to identify it, while HABITAT explains where it grows best. Plants valued by First Nation's peoples have an entry for NATIVE USE. In the LOCAL SITES section, I have listed a few good spots along the trail to admire each plant. Though these are some of the best areas, the lists are far from exhaustive. All the place names in the LOCAL SITES entries can be found in the maps on the front and back flaps.

Please note that, to keep the book pocket-sized, a few rare species and some plants found farther off the trail have not been included. The hiker with a keen interest and a sharp eye can expect to discover more treasures.

— Collin Varner

Hole-in-the-Wall

ACKNOWLEDGEMENTS

This guide could not have been prepared without the help of many people. I would like to acknowledge and thank the following:

Bob Baden and Shirly Kapula for their friendship and for allowing us to use their Bamfield residence.

My hiking companions, whose humour (often at my expense) was much needed — Garth Ramsey, Mike Donat, David van Berckel, Kevin Marks and David Sutherland, whom I've had the pleasure of completing the trail with twice.

The employees and wardens at Parks Canada for all of their information and excellent stewardship of the trail.

Dr. Karel Klinka for his careful proofreading.

The University of British Columbia, with special thanks to David Smith and John Metras.

The great staff at Raincoast Books: Kevin Williams, Scott Steedman, Simone Doust, Ingrid Paulson and Marjolein Visser.

Merry Merridith for her help with the artwork.

Brenda O'Reilly for her keyboarding skills.

And finally, to my wife, Wendy, and my daughter, Amber — my best supporters.

TWINFLOWER
Linnaea borealis • Honeysuckle family: *Caprifoliaceae*

■ **DESCRIPTION** Twinflower is an attractive trailing evergreen to 10 cm in height. Its nodding pink flowers are fragrant, to 5 mm long, and borne in pairs at the end of slender, Y-shaped stems. The evergreen leaves are 1 cm long, oval, shiny dark green above and paler below, with minute teeth on the upper half. The genus *Linnaea* is named for Carolus Linnaeus, Swedish botanist and founder of the binomial system for plant and animal classification. Twinflower is said to have been his favourite flower.

11

■ **HABITAT** Common in low to mid elevation forests across Canada.

■ **LOCAL SITES** Fragrant masses carpet the trail sides between the Klanawa River and Nitinat Narrows and the sides of the boardwalk from the Cheewhat River to Nitinat Narrows. Flowers mid-June through July.

The Red Creek Fir, a giant Douglas fir near Port Renfrew

OXEYE DAISY

Chrysanthemum leucanthemum • Aster family: *Asteraceae*

■ **DESCRIPTION** Oxeye daisy is an aromatic herbaceous perennial to 75 cm tall. Its flowers have the typical daisy white ray petals and yellow centre disks, to 5 cm across. The basal leaves are obovate with rounded teeth; the stem leaves are similar, though alternate. This is a European introduction that has naturalized on most of Vancouver Island and the Lower Mainland. "Chrysanthemum" is from the Greek *chrysos* ("gold") and *anthos* ("flower").

■ **HABITAT** Fields, meadows, very common on roadsides.

■ **LOCAL SITES** Common in Port Renfrew and Bamfield areas. Flowers June through July.

12

COLTSFOOT
Petasites palmatus • Aster family: *Asteraceae*

■ DESCRIPTION Coltsfoot is a large-leafed herbaceous perennial to 60 cm in height. Its purplish white flowers emerge before the leaves in late winter; they are grouped together to form terminal clusters approximately 10 cm across on a 60-cm stalk. The leaves have 7-9 lobes and grow to 30 cm across, green above and white and woolly below. The genus name *Petasites* is from the Greek word *petasos*, meaning "hat." Japanese children once used the large leaves as hats.

■ HABITAT Moist to wet areas at low to mid elevations.

■ NATIVE USE The leaves were used to cover berries in steam cooking pits.

■ LOCAL SITES Patchy at Red Creek and Carmanah Creek, lots at Darling Creek. Can also be seen at the top of Nitinat Lake and Cowichan Lake.

WESTERN FALSE ASPHODEL
Tofieldia glutinosa • Lily family: *Liliaceae*

■ **DESCRIPTION** Western false asphodel is a herbaceous perennial to 50 cm in height. Its creamy-white flowers are 1 cm across and borne in terminal clusters on long thin stems. The plump fruit capsules are reddish purple, spongy and very noticeable. The leaves are basal and grass-like. The species name *glutinosa* means "sticky," referring to the sticky upper portions of the stem. Bees and other flying insects can only access the flowers.

■ **HABITAT** Peat bogs at low to high elevations and wet alpine meadows.

14

■ **LOCAL SITES** Elevated bogs between Cullite Creek and Walbran Creek and on the wet cliff faces north of Tsusiat Falls. Flowers June and July.

YARROW
Achillea millefolium • Aster family: *Asteraceae*

■ **DESCRIPTION** Yarrow is a herbaceous perennial to 1 m in height. Its many small white flowers form flat-topped clusters 5-10 cm across. The aromatic leaves are so finely dissected that they appear fern-like, hence its species name "a thousand leaves." The genus is named after Achilles, a hero of Greek mythology.

■ **HABITAT** Roadsides, wasteland, common at low to mid elevations.

■ **NATIVE USE** Infusions and poultices were made for cold remedies.

■ **LOCAL SITES** Scattered on rocky outcrops on the ocean side of the trail. Flowers start end of May.

PEARLY EVERLASTING
Anaphalis margaritacea • Aster family: *Asteraceae*

■ **DESCRIPTION** Pearly everlasting grows to 80 cm in height and produces heads of small yellowish flowers surrounded by dry white bracts. The leaves are lance-shaped, green above and covered with a white felt underneath. If picked before they go to seed, the flowers remain fresh-looking long after they are brought in.

■ **HABITAT** Common on disturbed sites, roadsides and rock outcrops.

■ **LOCAL SITES** Sporadic on the rocky exposed side of the trail. Flowering starts towards the end of July.

16

COAST BOYKINIA
Boykinia elata • Saxifrage family: *Saxifragaceae*

■ **DESCRIPTION** Coast boykinia is a herbaceous perennial to 60 cm in height. Its small white flowers are produced on long slender stalks 25-60 cm tall. The grass green leaves are somewhat heart-shaped with 5-7 lobes, to 8 cm across, and supported on long slender hairy stems. When in flower, boykinia is very attractive. The species name *elata* means "tall."

■ **HABITAT** Moist forests, wet cliff faces and streamsides at low to mid elevations.

17

■ **LOCAL SITES** Moist wooded areas along most of the trail. Flowers June and July.

FOAM FLOWER
Tiarella trifoliata • Saxifrage family: *Saxifragaceae*

■ **DESCRIPTION** Foam flower is a herbaceous perennial to 50 cm in height. Each wiry stem supports several tiny white flowers. The massed flowers are thought to resemble foam. The trifoliate leaves (to 7 cm across) are all basal except for one, located approximately halfway up the stem; this is good for identification. There is another species of foam flower (*T. unifoliata*) that is very similar except for its solid leaf.

■ **HABITAT** Shaded moist woods at low to mid elevations.
■ **LOCAL SITES** Common on the forested sections of the trail. Flowering starts mid-May and continues through July. The solid-leaf foam flower can also be seen.

SMALL-FLOWERED ALUMROOT
Heuchera micrantha • Saxifrage family: *Saxifragaceae*

■ **DESCRIPTION** Small-flowered alumroot is a perennial to 60 cm in height. Its small white flowers are abundant and held on scapes (stems) up to 60 cm tall. The heart-shaped leaves have long hairy stems and are basal. The leaves are slightly longer than they are broad and distinguish this plant from smooth alumroot (*H. glabra*), which has leaves that are broader than they are long. The name "alumroot" is given because the roots are very astringent.

■ **HABITAT** Wet cliff faces and stream banks at low to high elevations.

■ **LOCAL SITES** Patchy on shaded wet rock faces. Flowers by the beginning of June.

TWISTED STALK
Streptopus amplexifolius • Lily family: *Liliaceae*

■ **DESCRIPTION** Twisted stalk is a branching, herbaceous perennial, 1-2 m in height. Its greenish white flowers are 1 cm long and borne in leaf axils on slender twisted stalks. The fruit develops into a bright red oval berry to 1 cm long. The ovate leaves are alternate, 5-12 cm long. They clasp the stem directly, with no petiole; the species name *amplexifolius* means "clasping leaves." The flowers and fruit hang from the leaf axils along the branches. CAUTION: the berries are considered poisonous.

■ **HABITAT** Cool moist forests at low to high elevations.

■ **NATIVE USE** The plants were tied to the clothing or hair for their scent.

■ **LOCAL SITES** Common in moist forest areas, abundant between Tsocowis Creek and Pachena Bay. Flowers at the beginning of June.

WESTERN PINK FAWN LILY

Erythronium revolutum • Lily family: *Liliaceae*

■ **DESCRIPTION** Western pink fawn lily is a herbaceous perennial to 30 cm in height. The nodding pink flowers are adorned with golden anthers. The seed takes 5 to 7 years to form a corm and put up its first flower; picking of the flowers has greatly reduced the numbers of this plant. The leaves are basal, lance-shaped, to 20 cm long and mottled white to dark green.

■ **HABITAT** Open forests at low elevations, usually in sandy soil by rivers and streams.

■ **LOCAL SITES** On the sandy banks of Cullite Creek. Flowers April to May.

WESTERN TRILLIUM
Trillium ovatum • Lily family: *Liliaceae*

■ **DESCRIPTION** The western trillium's beautiful flowers are made up of 3 white petals, approximately 5 cm long, and 3 green sepals, elevated on a stem 30-50 cm tall. The flowers change from white to pink to a mottled purple before withering away. The dark green leaves, usually arranged in whorls of threes, are widely ovate and up to 15 cm long. Development, logging and over-picking have led to a dramatic decrease in wild trilliums. They are now protected by law.

■ **HABITAT** Moist forested areas in southern B.C. at lower elevations.

■ **NATIVE USE** The fleshy rhizomes were used for medicinal purposes.

■ **LOCAL SITES** Very common in the Red Creek area, especially by the Red Creek Fir, a giant Douglas fir (see photo on page 10). Can also be seen in the Bamfield area. Flowering starts at the beginning of April.

FALSE LILY OF THE VALLEY
Maianthemum dilatatum • Lily family: *Liliaceae*

■ **DESCRIPTION** False lily of the valley is a small herbaceous perennial to 30 cm in height. Its small white flowers appear in April/May, clustered on 5-10 cm spikes. The slightly fragrant flowers are quickly replaced by berries 6 mm across; the berries go through summer a speckled green and brown but turn ruby red by autumn. The dark green leaves are alternate, heart-shaped and slightly twisted, to 10 cm long. The genus name *Maianthemum* is from the Greek *Maios* ("May") and *anthemon* ("blossom").

■ **HABITAT** Moist coastal forests at low elevations.

■ **NATIVE USE** The berries were eaten but were not highly regarded.

■ **LOCAL SITES** Common in forested sections of the trail. The leaves emerge mid-March and form carpets by the time the flowers bloom in early May. Berries start showing mid-June.

TIGER LILY

Lilium columbianum • Lily family: *Liliaceae*

■ **DESCRIPTION** Tiger lily is an elegant herbaceous perennial to 1.5 m tall. Its drooping flowers go from deep yellow to bright orange. A vigorous plant can have 20 or more flowers. Shortly after the flower buds have opened, the tepals curve backwards to reveal maroon spots and anthers. The leaves are lance-shaped, usually in a whorl and 5-10 cm long. It is said that he or she who smells a tiger lily will develop freckles.

■ **HABITAT** Diverse range, including open forests, meadows, rock outcrops and the sides of logging roads, at low to sub-alpine elevations.

■ **NATIVE USE** The bulbs were boiled or steamed and eaten.

■ **LOCAL SITES** Bamfield area and beside logging roads around Nitinat Lake. Flowering starts mid-May.

SILVERWEED

Potentilla anserina ssp. *pacifica* • Rose family: *Rosaceae*

■ **DESCRIPTION** Silverweed only grows to 30 cm in height but can take over several hectares in favourable conditions. The yellow flowers are produced singly on a leafless stalk. The compound leaves reach 25 cm in length and have 9-19 toothed leaflets; they are bicoloured, grass green above and felty silver below, hence the common name. Silverweed spreads quickly thanks to its fast-growing stolons, which root at the nodes. The genus name *Potentilla* means "powerful," a reference to its medicinal properties.

■ **HABITAT** Saline marshes, meadows and wet run-off areas near the ocean.

■ **NATIVE USE** The cooked roots were an important food source.

■ **LOCAL SITES** In the Bamfield area and in freshwater-fed beach areas along the shoreline.

RED PAINTBRUSH
Castilleja sp. • Figwort family: *Scrophulariaceae*

■ **DESCRIPTION** The many species of paintbrush are difficult to distinguish. They range in height from 20 to 80 cm and there is frequent hybridization within their diverse growing range, making identification even harder. Red paintbrush is a perennial with small lance-shaped leaves. Its actual flowers are small and inconspicuous — it is the showy red bracts that attract all the attention.

■ **HABITAT** Low elevation grassy meadows and rocky outcrops to moist sub-alpine and alpine meadows.

■ **LOCAL SITES** Common on dry rocky outcrops between Owen Point and Valencia Bluffs. Flowers June and July.

LARGE-LEAFED AVENS
Geum macrophyllum • Rose family: *Rosaceae*

■ **DESCRIPTION** Large-leafed avens is a herbaceous perennial to 90 cm in height. Its bright yellow flowers resemble buttercups. They are approximately 6 mm across and are produced singularly or in small clusters. The unique round fruit has bristly bent protruding styles that catch on fur and clothing, an excellent way of dispersing the seed. The irregular-shaped larger leaves are 15-20 cm across, while the stem leaves are smaller and 3-lobed.

■ **HABITAT** Prefers moist soil in open forests and beside pathways, trails and roads at low elevations.

■ **NATIVE USE** The roots were boiled and used medicinally.

■ **LOCAL SITES** Can be seen in spotty patches in open areas by the trail and in abundance between Tsusiat Falls and the Klanawa River. Flowering starts at the end of April and continues irregularly through August.

GEUM MACROPHYLLUM

YELLOW MONKEY-FLOWER
Mimulus guttatus • Figwort family: *Scrophulariaceae*

■ **DESCRIPTION** Yellow monkey-flower can be annual or perennial; normally it self-seeds, disappears and then germinates as an annual in spring. It can grow to 80 cm in height. Its beautiful yellow flowers are 2-lipped, to 5 cm long, with many small and one larger dot on the lower lip. The lower leaves are oval and grow in pairs, while the upper leaves hug the stem. Chickweed monkey-flower (*M. alsinoides*) is smaller, to 20 cm high, and often grows with the larger variety; its flowers are much smaller and have only a single dot on the lower lip.

■ **HABITAT** Wet cliffs and ledges at low elevations.

■ **LOCAL SITES** Common on damp cliff faces and ridges. Large drifts between Owen Point and Camper Creek. Flowers May to July.

COW-PARSNIP or INDIAN CELERY
Heracleum lanatum • Carrot family: *Apiaceae*

■ **DESCRIPTION** Cow-parsnip is a tall hollow-stemmed herbaceous perennial from 1 to 3 m in height. Its small white flowers are grouped in flat-topped umbrella-like terminal clusters to 25 cm across. It produces numerous small, egg-shaped seeds, 1 cm long, with a pleasant aroma. The large woolly compound leaves are divided into 3 leaflets, 1 terminal and 2 lateral (to 30 cm across). The genus name *Heracleum* is fitting for this plant of Herculean proportions. Giant cow-parsnip (*H. mantegazzianum*), an introduced species, grows to 4 m in height and can be seen in urban areas.

CAUTION: both species can cause severe blistering and rashes when handled.

■ **HABITAT** Moist forests, meadows, marshes and roadsides from low to high elevations.

■ **LOCAL SITES** Common on the forested edge of the trail. Flowering starts beginning of June.

WILD CARROT or QUEEN ANNE'S LACE
Daucus carota • Carrot family: *Apiaceae*

■ **DESCRIPTION** Wild carrot is an introduced biennial to 1 m in height. Its small white flowers are grouped together to form showy terminal clusters to 10 cm across. The leaves (to 15 cm long) are dissected to the point that they resemble delicate ferns. If the stems are scratched, a carrot scent is released. Wild carrot and parsnips have long been cultivated in Europe for culinary and medicinal use; records of them date back to 500 B.C.

32

■ **HABITAT** Roadsides, abandoned fields and highway medians at low elevations.

■ **LOCAL SITES** Common around Port Renfrew and Bamfield. Flowers July through September.

WATER-PARSLEY
Oenanthe sarmentosa • Carrot family: *Apiaceae*

■ **DESCRIPTION** Water-parsley is a semi-aquatic herbaceous perennial to 1 m in height. Its flowers are white, faintly fragrant and borne in flat-topped clusters. The leaves are pinnately divided 2-3 times, with deeply toothed leaflets. The overall appearance of the plant is weak and sprawling.

CAUTION: the entire plant is considered poisonous.

■ **HABITAT** Low-elevation marshes and swamps, occasionally in ditches.

■ **LOCAL SITES** Common in wet forest areas along the trail. Flowers mid-June through July.

33

COOLEY'S HEDGE-NETTLE
Stachys cooleyae • Mint family: *Lamiaceae*

■ **DESCRIPTION** Cooley's hedge-nettle is a herbaceous perennial to 1 m in height. Its purply red flowers are trumpet-like with a lower lip; they grow to 4 cm long and are grouped in terminal clusters. The leaves are mint-like with toothed edges, opposite, finely hairy on both sides, to 15 cm long. The stems are square and finely hairy. Cooley's hedge-nettle was first documented in 1891 by Grace Cooley, a professor from New Jersey who saw it near Nanaimo.

■ **HABITAT** Moist open forests and streamsides at low elevations.

■ **LOCAL SITES** Sporadic on the forest side of the trail, larger patches in moist flat areas at Darling River and up Carmanah Creek. Flowers in June to mid-July.

HEAL-ALL or SELF-HEAL
Prunella vulgaris • Mint family: *Lamiaceae*

■ **DESCRIPTION** Heal-all is an introduced herbaceous perennial to 40 cm in height. Its purple flowers are 2-lipped, 1-2 cm long, and borne in terminal spikes. The leaves are mostly lance-shaped, opposite, to 7 cm long. The stems are square. As its name suggests, heal-all has long been used medicinally. The seventeenth-century herbalist Nicholas Culpeper prescribed that it be "taken inwardly in syrups for inward wounds, outwardly in unguents and plasters for outward."

■ **HABITAT** Roadsides, forest edges, fields and parks at low elevations.
■ **LOCAL SITES** Spotty through open forest sections. Flowers most of the summer.

CREEPING BUTTERCUP
Ranunculus repens • Buttercup family: *Ranunculaceae*

■ **DESCRIPTION** Creeping buttercup is a prostrate creeping perennial that rarely grows above 30 cm in height. The flowers are 2-3 cm across; their solid deep yellow colour contrasts well with the dark green foliage. The pale blotched leaves have long stalks and are divided into 3 leaflets. CAUTION: they may not look threatening, but buttercups are considered poisonous and can cause skin irritations.

■ **HABITAT** Moist to wet sites in urban areas, parks, fields and open forests.

■ **LOCAL SITES** Mainly seen in Bamfield and Port Renfrew but also in settled areas along and off the trail. The taller wood buttercup (*R. uncinatus*) can be seen beside the boardwalk between the Cheewhat River and Nitinat Narrows.

RED COLUMBINE
Aquilegia formosa • Buttercup family: *Ranunculaceae*

■ **DESCRIPTION** Red columbine is a herbaceous perennial to 1 m in height. The drooping red-and-yellow flowers are up to 5 cm across and have 5 scarlet spurs arching backwards; they are almost translucent when the sun shines on them. The leaves are sea green above, paler below, to 8 cm across and twice divided by threes. In the head of the flower is a honey gland that can only be reached by hummingbirds and long-tongued butterflies. The hole that can sometimes be seen above this gland is caused by frustrated bumblebees chewing their way to the nectar. The name "columbine" means "dove," for the five arching spurs said to resemble five doves sitting around a dish.

■ **HABITAT** Moist open forests, meadows and creeksides at low to high elevations.

■ **LOCAL SITES** On rock ledges at Owen Point and creekside at Camper Creek. Flowers June to mid-July.

FALSE BUGBANE
Trautvetteria caroliniensis •
Buttercup family: *Ranunculaceae*

■ **DESCRIPTION** False bugbane is a large-leafed perennial
50-80 cm in height that spreads freely by rhizomes. Its
white flowers have sepals but no petals — the fuzzy-looking
flowers are actually stamens. These are held up in flat-
topped terminal clusters to 80 cm in height. The basal
leaves are maple-shaped, deeply divided into 5 lobes and
from 15 to 30 cm across. The stem leaves are smaller.
The genus is named for 19th century Russian botanist
E. R. von Trautvetter.

38

■ **HABITAT** Moist forests, floodplains
and streamsides at low to mid
elevations.

■ **LOCAL SITES** Port Renfrew trailhead, Red Creek, Camper Creek and
Carmanah Creek. Flowers mid-June
to mid-July.

WESTERN STAR FLOWER
Trientalis latifolia • Primrose family: *Primulaceae*

■ **DESCRIPTION** Western star flower is a small, herbaceous perennial 10-25 cm in height. Its white to pink flowers hang on very thin stalks, making them appear like stars. The oval leaves (5-10 cm long) are elevated in a whorl just under the flower stalks. There is a northern star flower (*T. arctica*) that is more confined to bogs and swamps; it is shorter (5-20 cm in height), with white flowers 1.5 cm across and additional leaves on the stem below the whorl of elevated leaves.

■ **HABITAT** Dry to moist coniferous forests at low elevations.

■ **LOCAL SITES** There are small patches just before Owen Point coming from Camper Creek. Flowering starts mid-May. Northern star flower can be seen in the elevated bogs between Cullite Creek and Walbran Creek. Flowering starts in June and continues through July.

FIREWEED
Epilobium angustifolium•
Evening primrose family: *Onagraceae*

■ **DESCRIPTION** Fireweed is a tall herbaceous perennial that reaches heights of 3 m in good soil. Its purply red flowers grow on long showy terminal clusters. The leaves are alternate, lance-shaped like a willow's, 10-20 cm long and darker green above than below. The minute seeds are produced in pods 5-10 cm long and have silky hairs for easy wind dispersal. Fireweed flowers have long been a beekeeper's favourite. The name "fireweed" comes from the fact that it is one of the first plants to grow on burned sites; typically follows wildfires.

■ **HABITAT** Common throughout B.C. in open areas and burned sites.
■ **NATIVE USE** The stem fibres were twisted into twine and made into fishing nets, and the fluffy seeds were used in padding and weaving.
■ **LOCAL SITES** Common in Port Renfrew and Red Creek areas, patchy along the sides of the trail. Flowers from mid-June to August.

BUNCHBERRY or DWARF DOGWOOD
Cornus canadensis • Dogwood family: *Cornaceae*

■ **DESCRIPTION** Bunchberry, a perennial no higher than 20 cm, is a reduced version of the Pacific dogwood tree (*C. nuttallii*). The tiny greenish flowers are surrounded by 4 showy white bracts, just like the flowers of the larger dogwood. The evergreen leaves, 4-7 cm long, grow in whorls of 5-7 and have parallel veins like the larger tree's. The beautiful red berries form in bunches (hence the name) just above the leaves in August. Bunchberry and Pacific dogwood have a habit of flowering twice, once in spring and again in late summer.

■ **HABITAT** From low to high elevations in cool moist coniferous forests and bogs.

■ **LOCAL SITES** Common by the trail, especially in boggy areas, where the flowers get so thick that they bubble over the sides of the boardwalks.

SKUNK CABBAGE

Lysichiton americanum • Arum family: *Araceae*

■ **DESCRIPTION** Skunk cabbage is a herbaceous perennial to 1.5 m in height and as much as 2 m across. The small greenish flowers are densely packed on a fleshy spike and surrounded by a showy yellow spathe, the emergence of which is a sure sign that spring is near. The tropical-looking leaves can be over 1 m long and 50 cm wide.

■ **HABITAT** Common at lower elevations in wet areas such as springs, swamps, seepage areas and floodplains.

■ **NATIVE USE** Skunk cabbage roots were cooked and eaten in spring in times of famine. It is said this poorly named plant has saved the lives of thousands.

■ **LOCAL SITES** Common in moist and wet areas along the entire trail.

SIBERIAN MINER'S LETTUCE
Claytonia sibirica • Purslane family: *Portulacaceae*

■ **DESCRIPTION** Siberian miner's lettuce is a small annual to 30 cm in height. Its small white to pink flowers are 5-petalled and produced in abundance on long, thin, fleshy stems. The basal leaves are long-stemmed, opposite, ovate and, like the stems, succulent. Another species, *C. perfoliata*, differs in that its upper leaves are disc-shaped and fused to other flower stems. Siberian miner's lettuce was first discovered in Russia, where it was a staple food for miners. Early prospectors and settlers found both species made excellent early-season salad greens.

■ **HABITAT** Moist forest areas at low to mid elevations.

■ **LOCAL SITES** Both species are common on the forested side of the trail. Flowering starts late April and continues through July.

VANILLA LEAF

Achlys triphylla • Barberry family: *Berberidaceae*

■ **DESCRIPTION** Vanilla leaf is a herbaceous perennial to 30 cm in height. Its small white flowers are formed on a spike that stands above the leaf. The small fruit (achenes) is crescent-shaped and greenish to reddish purple. The wavy leaves have long stems and are divided into 3 leaflets, one at each side and the third at the tip. When dried, the leaves have a faint vanilla-like scent.

■ **HABITAT** Dry to moist forests at low to mid elevations in southern B.C.

■ **NATIVE USE** The leaves were used as an insect repellent.

■ **LOCAL SITES** Like a ground cover in the Red Creek area, patchy around Bamfield. Flowers June to July.

SWAMP GENTIAN

Gentiana douglasiana • Gentian family: *Gentianaceae*

■**DESCRIPTION** Swamp gentian is a showy annual to 25 cm in height. Its white, symmetrical flowers grow to 1.5 cm across and are usually solitary. The stem leaves are elliptic, opposite, to 1 cm long, with the basal leaves sitting in a rosette. The genus is named after King Gentius of Illyria (2nd century B.C.), who is said to have discovered the medicinal properties of these plants.

■**HABITAT** Bogs and wet meadows at low to high elevations.

■**LOCAL SITES** Scattered in the elevated bog between Cullite Creek and Logan Creek, close to the boardwalk. Flowers mid-June to mid-July.

SALMONBERRY

Rubus spectabilis • Rose family: *Rosaceae*

■**DESCRIPTION** Salmonberry is one of B.C.'s tallest native berry bushes. Though it averages 2-3 m, the bush can grow up to 4 m high. The pink bell-shaped flowers, 3-4 cm across, bloom at the end of February and are a welcome sight. Flowering continues until June, when both the flowers and ripe fruit can be seen on the same bush. The soft logan-shaped berries range in colour from yellow to orange to red, with the occasional dark purple. The leaves are compound, with 3 leaflets, much like the leaves of a raspberry. Weak prickles may be seen on the lower portion of the branches; the tops are unarmed. The berry's common name comes from its resemblance to the shape and colour of salmon eggs.

■**HABITAT** Common on the coast of B.C. in shaded damp forests.

■**NATIVE USE** The high water content in the berries prevented them from being stored for any length of time. They were generally eaten shortly after harvesting.

■**LOCAL SITES** Common on the trail. Berries are harvested from mid-June to mid-July. One of the better picking spots on the trail is under the cable car ramp going up the Klanawa River.

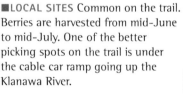

■DESCRIPTION Of B.C.'s three blackberry species, only one is native to the region. The two introduced species require more sunshine to thrive. The three are easy to identify:
Trailing blackberry (*Rubus ursinus*) — the first to bloom (end of April) and set fruit (mid-July), it is often seen rambling over plants in and out of forested areas. The berries are delicious and the leaves can be steeped as a tea.
Himalayan blackberry (*R. discolor*) — this blackberry was introduced from India and has now taken over much of the Pacific Northwest. It is heavily armed, grows rampant to 10 m and is a prolific producer of berries. Blooming starts mid-June and the fruit sets by mid-August.
Cutleaf blackberry (*R. laciniatus*) — introduced from Europe, this berry is very similar to the Himalayan blackberry but less common.
■HABITAT Common on open wasteland, forest edges and in ditches.

49

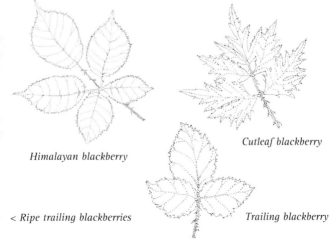

Himalayan blackberry

Cutleaf blackberry

< Ripe trailing blackberries

Trailing blackberry

SASKATOON BERRY or SERVICEBERRY
Amelanchier alnifolia • Rose family: *Rosaceae*

■**DESCRIPTION** Depending on growing conditions, the saskatoon berry can vary from a 1-m shrub to a small tree 7 m in height. The white showy flowers range from 1 to 3 cm across and often hang in pendulous clusters. The young reddish berries form early and by midsummer darken to a purple black up to 1 cm across. The light bluish green leaves are deciduous, oval-shaped and toothed above the middle.

■**HABITAT** Shorelines, rocky outcrops and open forests at low to mid elevations.

■**NATIVE USE** The berries were eaten fresh, mixed with other berries or dried for future use. On the great plains the berries were mashed with buffalo meat to make pemmican. The hard straight wood was a favourite for making arrows.

■**LOCAL SITES** Trailhead area in Port Renfrew, sporadic on rocky outcrops along the trail, good selection of berries on cliffs above Cheewhat and hugging the boardwalk in Bamfield. Flowering starts mid-April and the berries are fully ripe by the first week of August.

THIMBLEBERRY

Rubus parviflorus • Rose family: *Rosaceae*

■DESCRIPTION Thimbleberry is an unarmed shrub to 3 m in height. Its large white flowers open up to 5 cm across and are replaced by juicy bright red berries. The dome-shaped berries are 2 cm across and bear little resemblance to a thimble. The maple-shaped leaves grow up to 25 cm across and, when needed, make a good tissue substitute.

■HABITAT Common in coastal and interior B.C. in open forests at low to mid elevations.

■NATIVE USE The large leaves were used to line cooking pits and cover baskets. The berries were eaten fresh, dried or mixed with other berries.

■LOCAL SITES Common along the trail. Flowering starts mid-May and the fruit matures at the end of July or early August.

OVAL-LEAFED BLUEBERRY

Vaccinium ovalifolium • Heather family: *Ericaceae*

■**DESCRIPTION** The oval-leafed blueberry is one of B.C.'s most recognized and harvested blueberries. It is a mid-size bush to 2 m in height. The pinkish bell-shaped flowers appear before the leaves and are followed by the classic blueberries. Rubbing the berries reveals a covering of dull bloom and a darker berry. The soft green leaves are smooth-edged, alternate, egg-shaped (no point) and grow to 4 cm in length.

■**HABITAT** Moist coniferous forests from sea level to high elevations.

■**NATIVE USE** Blueberries were a valuable and delicious food source. They were eaten fresh, mixed with other berries and dried for future use. As with all blueberries, they were also mashed to create a purple dye used to colour basket materials.

■**LOCAL SITES** Common in the moist forested areas of the trail with excellent picking spots around Camper Creek. Flowering starts mid-April and the fruit ripens as early as mid-June.

SALAL
Gaultheria shallon • Heather family: *Ericaceae*

■**DESCRIPTION** Salal is a prostrate to mid-size bush that grows from 0.5 to 4 m in height. In spring the small pinkish flowers (1 cm long) hang like strings of tiny Chinese lanterns. The edible dark purple berries grow to 1 cm across and ripen by mid-August to September. Both the flowers and berries display themselves for several weeks. The dark green leaves are 7-10 cm long, tough and oval-shaped. Salal is often overlooked by berry pickers; the ripe berries taste excellent fresh and make fine preserves and wine.

■**HABITAT** Dry to moist forested areas along the entire coast.

■**NATIVE USE** Salal was an important food source for most native peoples. The berries were eaten fresh, mixed with other berries, or crushed and placed on skunk cabbage leaves to dry. The dried berry cakes were then rolled up and preserved for winter use.

■**LOCAL SITES** Common understory bush. Flowering starts beginning of May, fruit starts to ripen beginning of August.

Arctostaphylos uva-ursi • Heather family: *Ericaceae*

■**DESCRIPTION** Kinnikinnick is a trailing, mat-forming evergreen that rarely grows above 25 cm in height. Its fragrant, pinkish flowers bloom in spring and are replaced by bright red berries 1 cm across by late summer. The small, oval leaves grow to 3 cm long, are leathery and alternate. Grouse and bears feed on the berries.

■**HABITAT** Dry rocky outcrops and well-drained forest areas throughout B.C., from sea level to high elevations.

■**NATIVE USE**
Kinnikinnick is an eastern native word used to describe a tobacco mix. The leaves were dried and smoked, sometimes mixed with other plants.

■**LOCAL SITES** Higher exposed elevations between Nitinat Narrows and Tsusiat Falls.

EVERGREEN HUCKLEBERRY
Vaccinium ovatum • Heather family: *Ericaceae*

■**DESCRIPTION** Evergreen huckleberry is an attractive, mid-size shrub to 3 m in height. In spring it is covered in clusters of pinkish bell-shaped flowers. By late summer the branches are weighed down by the many small blue-black berries (5-7 mm across). This is a favourite late-season bush among avid berry pickers.

■**HABITAT** Coniferous forests in southern coastal B.C., Vancouver Island and Gulf Islands.

■**NATIVE USE** The late-producing berries were in high demand for their flavour.

■**LOCAL SITES** Scattered along exposed portions of the trail. Large concentrations follow the boardwalk from the Cheewhat River to Nitinat Narrows. Flowering starts in early May and the berries ripen early September to December.

RED HUCKLEBERRY
Vaccinium parvifolium • Heather family: *Ericaceae*

■**DESCRIPTION** One of the most graceful of all B.C.'s berry bushes, the red huckleberry grows on old stumps, where it can attain heights of 3-4 m. The combination of almost translucent red berries (1 cm across), lacy zigzag branch structure and pale green leaves (oval, 2-5 cm long) is unmistakable. The small greenish to pink flowers are inconspicuous.

■**HABITAT** Coastal forested areas at lower elevations.

■**NATIVE USE** The berries were eaten fresh, mixed with other berries and dried for winter use. Their resemblance to salmon eggs made them ideal for fish bait.

■**LOCAL SITES** Common along forested areas of the trail. Flowering starts mid-April and the berries ripen by the beginning of July.

COASTAL STRAWBERRY

Fragaria chiloensis • Rose family: *Rosaceae*

■**DESCRIPTION** Coastal strawberry is a deciduous maritime perennial that grows to 30 cm in height. Its white flowers are 5-petalled, to 3 cm across, with approximately 20 orange stamens. The red fruit is small (1.5 cm across) and tasty. The leathery leaves are basal and divided into 3 leaflets that are obovate, coarsely toothed and woolly beneath. Strawberry leaves can be steeped to make a refreshing tea. The species name refers to this plant's extensive range, from Alaska to the coast of Chile.

■**HABITAT** Usually seen on exposed rocky outcrops or in sand near the ocean.

■**LOCAL SITES** Sporadic along the ocean side of the trail, with huge patches (2 m by 6 m) at Dare Beach. Flowers June and July.

LADY FERN

Athyrium filix-femina • Polypody family: *Polypodiaceae*

■**DESCRIPTION** Lady fern is a tall fragile fern to 2 m in height. The apple green fronds average up to 30 cm across and are widest below the centre, tapering at top and bottom. This diamond shape distinguishes the lady fern from the similar-looking spiny wood fern (*Dryopteris expansa*) whose fronds have an abrupt triangular form. The fronds die off in winter and emerge again in April. The horseshoe-shaped sori appear on the back of the fronds in spring.

■**HABITAT** Moist forests with nutrient-rich soils.

■**NATIVE USE** The young fronds (fiddleheads) were sometimes eaten in April.

■**LOCAL SITES** Common in the lower moist forested areas. A grove of lady ferns over 2 m in height gracefully arches over the trail between Klanawa River and Trestle Creek.

MAIDENHAIR FERN
Adiantum pedatum • Polypody family: *Polypodiaceae*

■**DESCRIPTION** Maidenhair fern is a delicate-looking fern with an almost tropical appearance. The fan-shaped fronds carry the dainty green leaflets (pinnules), which contrast well with the dark stems (stipes) that grow up to 60 cm in length. The reproducing sori under the pinnules are visible in late summer and fall. The genus name *Adiantum*, meaning "unwetted," refers to the way the fronds repel water.

■**HABITAT** Moist cliff faces at low to mid elevations.

■**NATIVE USE** The shiny black stipes were used in basket-making.

■**LOCAL SITES** Abundant on moist cliff faces. Can be seen growing alone or in masses from Owen Point to Michigan Creek and at Pachena Bay. There are large concentrations by Tsusiat Falls.

DEER FERN

Blechnum spicant • Polypody family: *Polypodiaceae*

■**DESCRIPTION** Deer fern can be distinguished from licorice fern (*Polypodium glycyrrhiza*) and sword fern (*Polystichum munitum*) by its two distinct types of frond, sterile and fertile. The sterile fronds grow up to 75 cm long, are tapered at both ends and usually lie flat. The fertile or spore-producing fronds are erect from the centre of the plant and can grow up to 75 cm in height. Deer ferns are good winter browse for deer.

■**HABITAT** Moist forested areas with plenty of rainfall.

■**LOCAL SITES** The most common fern on the trail, alone or as complete ground cover.

62

BRACKEN FERN

Pteridium aquilinum • Polypody family: *Polypodiaceae*

■**DESCRIPTION** Bracken fern is B.C.'s tallest native fern, often reaching 3 m or more in height. It is also the most widespread fern in the world. The tall, arching fronds are dark green with a golden green stem (stipe), triangular in shape, and grow singly from rhizomes in spring.

■**HABITAT** Has a diverse growing range, from dry to moist and open to forested regions.

■**NATIVE USE** The rhizomes were peeled and eaten fresh or cooked, and the fiddleheads were boiled and eaten. However, it is not advisable to eat this fern as it has now been proven to be a health hazard.

■**LOCAL SITES** Scattered along the trail.

63

SPINY WOOD FERN OR SHIELD FERN

Dryopteris expansa • Polypody family: *Polypodiaceae*

■**DESCRIPTION** Spiny wood fern is an elegant plant to 1.5 m tall. The pale green fronds are triangular in shape, average up to 25 cm across and die off in winter. In spring the rounded sori are produced on the underside of the fronds. Spiny wood fern is similar in appearance and requirements to lady fern (*Athyrium filix-femina*).

■**HABITAT** Common in moist forests at low to mid elevations.

■**LOCAL SITES** Common in cool, moist forested areas along the trail.

WESTERN SWORD FERN

Polystichum munitum • Polypody family: *Polypodiaceae*

■**DESCRIPTION** Western sword fern is southern B.C.'s most common fern. It is evergreen and can grow to 1.5 m in height. The fronds are dark green with side leaves (pinnae) that are sharply pointed and toothed. On the underside of the fronds a double row of sori forms midsummer and turns orange by autumn. The fronds are in high demand in eastern Canada for floral decorations. The species name *munitum* means "armed," referring to the side leaves that resemble swords.

■**HABITAT** Dry to moist forests at low elevations near the coast, where it can form pure groves.

■**NATIVE USE** The ferns were used to line steaming pits and baskets, and were placed on floors as sleeping mats.

■**LOCAL SITES** Common along forested sides of the trail.

LICORICE FERN
Polypodium glycyrrhiza • Polypody family: *Polypodiaceae*

■**DESCRIPTION** Licorice fern is a smaller evergreen fern commonly seen on mossy slopes and on the trunks of bigleaf maple trees. The dark green fronds grow to 50 cm long and 5-7 cm wide and have a golden stem (stipe). The round spores are produced in a single row under the leaves. The rhizomes have a licorice taste, hence the fern's common name.

■**HABITAT** Low-elevation forests, where it grows on trunks and branches of large trees, sometimes on shady outcrops.

■**NATIVE USE** The roots were eaten fresh or cooked and were also used as a cold and throat medicine.

■**LOCAL SITES** Small patches can be seen growing on trunks of red alder at Carmanah. The shorter species, leather leaf polypody (*P. scouleri*), is more leathery and round and can be seen growing on Sitka spruce trunks and cliff faces by the ocean at Tsusiat Falls and Pachena Point.

ROUND-LEAFED SUNDEW
Drosera rotundifolia • Sundew family: *Droseraceae*

■**DESCRIPTION** There are about 100 species of sundew around the world, and all of them eat insects. B.C.'s native round-leafed sundew is a small perennial, 5-25 cm high, with inconspicuous white flowers. It is the leaves that make this plant a curiosity. They are equipped with fine red hairs, each tipped with a shiny globe of reddish secretion. Small insects are attracted to the secretion and get stuck in it; the leaf then slowly folds over and smothers the unsuspecting visitors. The plant's favourite foods are mosquitoes, gnats and midges.

■**HABITAT** Peat bogs throughout the west coast of B.C.

■**NATIVE USE** The whole plant is acrid, and the leaves were once used to remove corns, warts and bunions.

■**LOCAL SITES** The elevated bog between Cullite Creek and Logan Creek is carpeted with sundew.

COMMON HORSETAIL
Equisetum arvense • Horsetail family: *Equisetaceae*

■**DESCRIPTION** Common horsetail is a herbaceous perennial to 75 cm in height. It has two types of stems, fertile and sterile, both hollow except at the nodes. The fertile stems are unbranched, to 30 cm in height, and lack chlorophyll; they bear spores in the terminal head. The green sterile stems grow to 75 cm in height and have leaves whorled at the joints. Horsetails are all that is left of a prehistoric family, some members of which grew to the size of trees.
■**HABITAT** Low wet seepage areas, meadows, damp sandy soils and gravel roads from low to high elevations.
■**LOCAL SITES** Bog edges and other damp areas on the forest side of the trail.

RUNNING CLUBMOSS
Lycopodium clavatum • Clubmoss family: *Lycopodiaceae*

■**DESCRIPTION** Running clubmoss is a curious creeping evergreen that looks like it is made of bright green pipe cleaners. Like all clubmosses, it has no flowers and reproduces by spores. These are held in terminal cones on vertical stalks to 25 cm in height. The evergreen leaves are lance-shaped and arranged spirally around the stem. Running clubmoss grows horizontally across the ground, with irregular rooting. The spores are used medicinally and in industry.

■**HABITAT** Dry to moist coniferous forests at low to high elevations.

■**LOCAL SITES** Higher elevations between Nitinat Narrows and Tsusiat Falls.

70

STINGING NETTLE
Urtica dioica • Nettle family: *Urticaceae*

■**DESCRIPTION** Stinging nettle is a herbaceous perennial to over 2 m in height. Its tiny flowers are greenish and produced in hanging clusters to 5 cm long. The leaves are heart-shaped at the base, tapered to the top, coarsely toothed, to 10 cm long. The stalks, stems and leaves all have stinging hairs that contain formic acid; many people have the misfortune of encountering this plant the hard way. The genus name *Urtica* is from the Latin *uro* ("to burn").

■**HABITAT** Thrives in moist, nutrient-rich, somewhat shady disturbed sites, where it can form great masses. Stinging nettles are usually an indicator of nitrogen-rich soil.

■**NATIVE USE** The young leaves were boiled as a spinach substitute.

■**LOCAL SITES** Large patches in rich soil areas at Carmanah Point and around Bamfield. Flowering starts at the beginning of May.

CLEAVER or BEDSTRAW
Galium aparine • Madder family: *Rubiaceae*

■**DESCRIPTION** Cleaver is a sprawling, clinging or climbing annual to 60 cm long. Its small white flowers are stalked from the leaf axils. The resulting fruit are annoying little burrs covered with hooked bristles. The bristly leaves are very narrow, to 5 cm long, and grow in whorls of 6-8. The back-angled bristles on the square stems and leaves help the plant to climb over and through other plants.

■**HABITAT** Most commonly seen near or on beaches, climbing over rocks and logs; on disturbed sites; and in broad-leafed forests.

■**NATIVE USE** The abrasive parts of the plant were rubbed between the hands to remove pitch.

■**LOCAL SITES** Common near sandy beaches, in association with dune grass. Flowers in spring, with the burrs maturing in July.

72

DEER CABBAGE
Fauria crista-galli • Buck bean family: *Menyanthaceae*

■**DESCRIPTION** Deer cabbage is a low-growing lush perennial to 50 cm in height. Its white flowers are split into 5 wavy lobes (petals), to 2 cm across, and sit in open clusters on stems 20-50 cm long. The leaves are basal, 7-12 cm across, rounded to heart-shaped, with bumpy edges (crenate). The species name *crista-galli* means "cockscomb," a reference to the wavy lobes.

■**HABITAT** Moist to wet forests, bogs and seepage areas at low to high elevations.

■**LOCAL SITES** Dominant ground cover in elevated bogs between Cullite Creek and Walbran Creek. Flowers mid-June through July.

NARROW-LEAFED COTTON GRASS
Eriophorum angustifolium • Sedge family: *Cyperaceae*

■DESCRIPTION Cotton grass is a rhizomatous herbaceous perennial to 70 cm in height. The inconspicuous flowers are held on triangular stems 30-70 cm long. When mature, the flowers are covered with silky white hairs (cotton) to 3 cm long. The flat leaves look like grass. The species name *angustifolium* means "narrow-leafed."

■HABITAT Peat bogs at low to high elevations; tolerates shallow water.

■LOCAL SITES Elevated bog between Cullite Creek and Logan Creek. Flowers June and July.

SEABEACH SANDWORT
Honkenya peploides • Pink family: *Caryophyllaceae*

■**DESCRIPTION** Seabeach sandwort is a herbaceous perennial to 30 cm in height. Its odd-looking flowers are greenish white, to 1.5 cm across and held in terminal leaf whorls. The fleshy leaves are elliptic, pale green, opposite, to 5 cm long. Sandwort can be seen growing as a single plant or as a mat to 1 m across. The genus name is after G. Honckeny, an 18th-century German botanist.

■**HABITAT** Upper sandy beaches, between rocks and logs.

■**LOCAL SITES** Scattered along sandy beaches, good concentrations at Dare Beach and Michigan Creek. Flowers June and July.

DUNE GRASS

Elymus mollis • Grass family: *Poaceae*

■**DESCRIPTION** Dune grass is a clump-forming perennial to 1.5 m in height. Its flowers are borne in wheat-like spikes to 30 cm long. The leaf blades are tough, usually folded, fuzzy above, smooth below, to 1.5 cm wide. The genus name is from *elymos*, the Greek name for millet. *Mollis* means "soft."

■**HABITAT** Coastal sandy beaches, where it often grows several metres into the forest.

76

■**NATIVE USE** The leaves and stems were used to make baskets.

■**LOCAL SITES** Sandy beaches along the trail.

BULL KELP

Nereocystis luetkeana • Brown alga family: *Phaeophyceae*

■**DESCRIPTION** Bull kelp is B.C.'s largest marine alga, to 30 m in length. It is held on the ocean floor by root-like holdfasts. At this point the stalk is very thin, but it increases in diameter until it terminates in a bulbous float to 15 cm wide. Attached to the float are clusters of brownish leaf-like blades to 4.5 m long.

■**HABITAT** Ocean outside the low tide zone, usually in at least 6 m of water with a rocky bottom. In protected areas it can form several hectares of beds.

■**NATIVE USE** The floats were used as containers to hold eulachon grease, fish oil and, more recently, molasses. The thin stalks were made into fishing lines, nets and rope.

■**LOCAL SITES** Individual plants can be seen washed up on shore. The largest beds are at Carmanah.

SLOUGH SEDGE
Carex obnupta • Sedge family: *Cyperaceae*

■**DESCRIPTION** Slough sedge is a wetland plant to 1.5 m in height. Its inflorescence (flower-head) is made up of dark brown male and female drooping spikes. The leaves are typically grass-like and not as long as the flowering stem.

■**HABITAT** Wet meadows, swamps, marshes and lake edges at lower elevations.

■**NATIVE USE** Slough sedge was and still is an important

basket-weaving material. The leaves are gathered in

summer, split in half, then hung to dry and bundled for fall and winter use.

■**LOCAL SITES** Beside the boardwalk over the swamp between Tsusiat Falls and the Klanawa River.

SILVER BURWEED

Ambrosia chamissonis • Aster family: *Asteraceae*

■**DESCRIPTION** Silver burweed is a coastal herbaceous perennial to 1 m in height/length. Its flowers are separate, with males in terminal heads and females in the lower leaf axils. The felty leaves are deeply divided, silvery green, to 7 cm long.

■**HABITAT** Coastal sandy beaches, between logs and rocks.

■**LOCAL SITES** Sprawling around large driftwood at Dare Point.

AMERICAN SEAROCKET
Cakile edentula • Mustard family: *Brassicaceae*

■**DESCRIPTION** American searocket is a coastal sprawling annual to 50 cm in height/length. Its pink to mauve flowers form towards the end of the stems and are up to 8 cm long. The odd-looking leaves are oblong, to 7 cm long and, like the stems, fleshy. When ripe, the pod-like fruit break up easily in the waves.

■**HABITAT** Coastal sandy beaches, prefers long shallow tides.

■**LOCAL SITES** Sandy coves and bays. Flowers mid-June through July.

ROCKWEED OR POPPING WRACK
Fucus sp. • Brown alga family: *Phaeophyceae*

■**DESCRIPTION** Rockweed is an intertidal seaweed (alga) from 15 to 60 cm in length. Its branches are flat, brown, leathery and thick through the middle, with inflated ends. It attaches itself to intertidal rocks with a small, disc-like holdfast.
■**HABITAT** Rocky beaches along the coastline.
■**NATIVE USE** Children used to step on the swollen ends to make them pop — hence the common name "popping wrack." On hot days, fishermen placed rockweed over their catch to keep it cool.
■**LOCAL SITES** Common on rocky beaches.

SEA PLANTAIN
Plantago maritima ssp. *juncoides* •
Plantain family: *Plantaginaceae*

DESCRIPTION Sea plantain is a coastal beach perennial to 30 cm in height. Its flowers are typical of plantain — small, greenish and tightly grouped on stiff spikes to 30 cm. The leaves are pale green, fleshy, basal, erect and slightly shorter than the flower spikes. Its sharp leaves and flower spikes make this plant easy to recognize.
HABITAT Sandy ocean shorelines and saline marshes.
LOCAL SITES Grows in cracks of large rocks by the high tide line.

NOOTKA ROSE

Rosa nutkana • Rose family: *Rosaceae*

■**DESCRIPTION** The largest of B.C.'s native roses, the Nootka rose grows to 3 m in height. The showy pink flowers are 5-petalled, fragrant, 5 cm across and usually solitary. The compound leaves have 5-7 toothed leaflets and are armed with a pair of prickles underneath. The reddish hips are round and plump, 1-2 cm across, and contrast well with the dark green foliage.

■**HABITAT** Open low-elevation forests throughout B.C.

■**NATIVE USE** Rosehips were strung together to make necklaces and the flowers were pressed to make perfume. Rosehips were only eaten in times of famine.

■**LOCAL SITES** Commonly seen as single bushes or thickets 2.5-m-high, mainly on exposed areas of the trail. Flowers begin mid-May and the hips start to develop colour by the beginning of August.

GOAT'S BEARD
Aruncus dioicus • Rose family: *Rosaceae*

■**DESCRIPTION** Goat's beard is a deciduous shrub to 3 m in height. The plants are dioecious — male and female flowers appear on separate plants. The tiny white flowers are compacted into hanging panicles up to 60 cm long. The leaves are compound 3 times (thrice pinnate); leaflets are bright green with a toothed edge, tapering to a point. With a little imagination, the hanging flowers can look like a goat's beard.

■**HABITAT** Moist open woodlands, creeksides and wet rocky slopes at lower elevations.

■**LOCAL SITES** Common in lightly forested areas and on the ocean side of the trail. Flowers June and early July.

DEVIL'S CLUB
Oplopanax horridus • Ginseng family: *Araliaceae*

■**DESCRIPTION** Devil's club is a deciduous shrub from 1-3 m in height. Its small white flowers are densely packed into pyramidal clusters approximately 15 cm long. The flowers bloom in May and are replaced by showy scarlet berries in August; these are not considered edible. The large leaves are maple-like, alternate, to 30 cm across, with spines in the larger veins on both sides. The stems are sprawling, awkward-looking and very well-armed with spines to 1 cm long. The species name *horridus* comes to mind when you accidentally encounter this shrub.

■**HABITAT** Moist forested areas with rich soil at low to mid elevations.

■**NATIVE USE** Next to hellebore, devil's club was coastal natives' most valued medicinal plant. Infusions and poultices were used to relieve arthritis, fevers, colds and infections.

■**LOCAL SITES** Around Bamfield area.

RED-BERRIED ELDER or RED ELDERBERRY
Sambucus racemosa • Honeysuckle family: *Caprifoliaceae*

■**DESCRIPTION** Red-berried elder is a bushy shrub to 6 m in height. Its small flowers are creamy-white and grow in pyramidal clusters 10-20 cm long. The berries that replace them take up to 3 months to turn bright red; they are considered poisonous to people when eaten raw but are a favourite food for birds. The leaves are compound, 5-15 cm long, with 5-9 opposite leaflets.

CAUTION: the berries are considered poisonous.

■**HABITAT** Moist coastal forest edges and roadsides. The blue-berried elder (*S. caerulea*) is found more in the Interior and the Gulf Islands.

■**NATIVE USE** The pithy branches were hollowed out and used as blowguns.

■**LOCAL SITES** Common in forested areas, berries ripen late June to July.

SNOWBERRY

Symphoricarpos albus • Honeysuckle family: *Caprifoliaceae*

■**DESCRIPTION** Snowberry is an erect deciduous shrub to 2 m in height. Its small white to pink flowers turn into an abundance of very noticeable white berries 1-2 cm across. Older plants produce a smaller oval leaf to 2 cm long, while younger, more vigorous plants have wavy leaves to 5 cm long. The leaves have a sweet fragrance when wet. Snowberries are best appreciated in winter, when the bright white berries stand out against the surrounding grey. The genus name *Symphoricarpos* refers to the clustering of the berries.

CAUTION: the berries are considered poisonous.

■**HABITAT** Open forested areas at low to mid elevations.

■**NATIVE USE** Thin branches were hollowed out to make pipe stems and larger branches were bound together to make brooms.

■**LOCAL SITES** Scattered patches along forested side of trail. Not noticeable until the white berries form in September.

BLACK TWINBERRY
Lonicera involucrata • Honeysuckle family: *Caprifoliaceae*

■DESCRIPTION Black twinberry is a deciduous shrub 1-3 m in height. Its yellow flowers are tubular and borne in pairs, to 2 cm long. The inedible berries are shiny black, cupped in a moon bract, to 1 cm across. The leaves are broadly lance-shaped, tapering to a point, opposite, 5-15 cm long.

■HABITAT Moist to wet open forests, at low to high elevations.

■NATIVE USE The berries were mashed and the purple juice used to dye roots for basketry. The Haida rubbed the berries directly into their scalps to prevent their hair turning grey. It was said that eating the berries drove a person crazy.

■LOCAL SITES Common along the trail, can be seen as a singular plant or as impenetrable thickets 3 m tall. A black twinberry of tree-like proportions can be seen on the cliff at Carmanah Point, about 500 m from Chez Monique's. Flowering starts mid-May, with the berries appearing mid-June.

FALSE AZALEA or FOOL'S HUCKLEBERRY
Menziesia ferruginea • Heather family: *Ericaceae*

■DESCRIPTION False azalea is an upright, deciduous shrub to 3 m in height. Its flowers, which resemble a huckleberry's, are a dull copper colour, bell-shaped, to 8 mm long, with long stems. The small fruit (5 mm long) is a dry, four-valved capsule that is not edible. The leaves are elliptic, bluish green on top, whitish green below, 3-6 cm long. They appear to grow in whorls. The genus name *Menziesia* is after Archibald Menzies, a naval surgeon and botanist who sailed with Captain George Vancouver and collected plants on the West Coast.

■HABITAT Moist forested sites, especially in wetter areas at low to high elevations.

■LOCAL SITES Common in moist forested areas along the trail.

WESTERN BOG LAUREL
Kalmia microphylla ssp. *occidentalis* • Heather family: *Ericaceae*

■**DESCRIPTION** B.C.'s native laurel is a small lanky evergreen no more than 60 cm high. Its beautiful pink flowers (2.5 cm across) have a built-in pollen dispenser. A close look reveals that some of the stamens are bent over; these spring up when the flower is disturbed, dusting the intruder with pollen. The leaves are opposite, lance-shaped, 2-4 cm long, shiny dark green above, felty white below, with edges strongly rolled over. The plant is poisonous and should not be confused with Labrador tea (*Ledum groenlandicum*; see opposite), which it resembles from above. CAUTION: the plant is poisonous.

■**HABITAT** Peat bogs, lakeshores, low to high elevations throughout B.C.

■**NATIVE USE** The leaves were boiled and used in small doses for medicinal purposes.

■**LOCAL SITES** Extensive patches in elevated bog between Cullite Creek and Logan Creek, among the dominant shore pines. Flowers early May.

LABRADOR TEA

Ledum groenlandicum • Heather family: *Ericaceae*

■**DESCRIPTION** Most of the year, Labrador tea is a gangly small shrub to 1.4 m in height. In spring the masses of small white flowers turn it into the Cinderella of the bog. The evergreen leaves are lance-shaped, alternate, 4-6 cm long, with the edges rolled over. The leaves can be distinguished from those of the poisonous bog laurel (*Kalmia microphylla*; see opposite) by their flat green colour on top and rusty-coloured hairs beneath. To be safe, only pick the leaves when the shrub is in flower.

■**HABITAT** Peat bogs, lakesides and permanent wet meadows, low to alpine elevations.

■**NATIVE USE** The leaves have long been used by native groups across Canada as infusions. Early explorers and settlers quickly picked up on this caffeine substitute. Caution must be taken — not all people can drink it.

■**LOCAL SITES** Elevated bog between Logan Creek and Walbran Creek. This bog is dominated by Labrador tea, stunted shore pine and deer cabbage. Flowering starts mid-May.

BIGLEAF MAPLE
Acer macrophyllum • Maple family: *Aceraceae*

■DESCRIPTION The bigleaf maple is the largest native maple on the West Coast, often exceeding heights of 30 m. Its huge leaves, which are dark green, 5-lobed, 20-30 cm across, are excellent identifiers. In early spring it produces beautiful clusters of scented yellow-green flowers, 7-10 cm long. The mature winged seeds (samaras), 5 cm long, act as whirlygigs when they fall; they are bountiful and an important food source for birds, squirrels, mice and chipmunks. The brown fissured bark is host to an incredible number of epiphytes, most commonly mosses and licorice ferns (see page 66).

■HABITAT Dominant in lower forested areas. Its shallow root system prefers moist soils, mild winters and cool summers.

■NATIVE USE The plentiful wood was important in native culture, as a fuel and for carvings, paddles, combs, fish lures, dishes and handles. The large leaves were used to line berry baskets and steam pits.

■LOCAL SITES Found inland from the coast, such as towards the end of Nitinat Lake. B.C.'s tallest recorded bigleaf maple, 31.7 m, is in Stanley Park. Flowers mid-April.

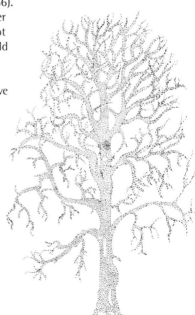

RED ALDER
Alnus rubra • Birch family: *Betulaceae*

■**DESCRIPTION** The largest native alder in North America, the red alder grows quickly and can reach 25 m in height. Its leaves are oval-shaped, grass green, 7-15 cm long, with a coarsely serrated edge. Hanging male catkins, 7-15 cm long, decorate the bare trees in early spring. The fruit (cones) are 1.5 to 2.5 cm long; they start off green, then turn brown and persist through winter. The bark is thin and grey on younger trees, scaly when older. Red alder leaves give a poor colour display in autumn, mainly green or brown.

■**HABITAT** Moist wooded areas, disturbed sites and stream banks at low to mid elevations.

■**NATIVE USE** The soft straight-grained wood is easily worked and was used for making masks, bowls, rattles, paddles and spoons. The red bark was used to dye fishnets, buckskins and basket material.

■**LOCAL SITES** The red alder is the dominant deciduous tree on the trail, in both forested and exposed beach areas. B.C.'s tallest recorded red alder, 41 m, is at Third Beach in Stanley Park.

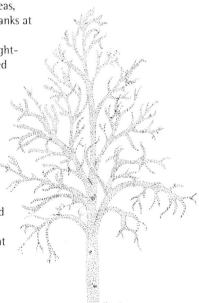

CASCARA
Rhamnus purshiana • Buckthorn family: *Rhamnaceae*

■DESCRIPTION Cascara can be a multi-trunked shrub or a small tree to 9 m in height. Its leaves are oblong with prominent veins, glossy, grass green, 7-13 cm long. The flowers are small, greenish yellow and rather insignificant. The berries look like small cherries, 1-8 mm across, red at first, turning blue black in late summer. The smooth bark is silver grey and on older trees it resembles an elephant's hide. The bark was collected commercially for years and used as the key ingredient in laxatives.
■HABITAT Prefers moist, nutrient-rich soil in the shade of larger trees at low elevations.
■NATIVE USE The bark was boiled and the infusion used as a laxative.
■LOCAL SITES Scattered small trees between Port Renfrew and Bamfield, larger trees 8 m high in Bamfield area.

PACIFIC CRAB APPLE

Malus fusca • Rose family: *Rosaceae*

■**DESCRIPTION** Pacific crab apple is a deciduous shrub or small tree 2-10 m high. Its leaves (5-10 cm long) are similar to those of orchard apple trees, except that they often have bottom lobes. The flowers are typical apple blossoms, white to pink, fragrant and in clusters of 5-12. The fruit that follows is 1-2 cm across, green at first, turning yellowy reddish. On older trees the bark is scaly and deeply fissured. The Pacific crab apple is B.C.'s only native apple.

■**HABITAT** High beaches, moist open forests, swamps and stream banks at lower elevations.

■**NATIVE USE** The small apples were an important food source, and the hard wood was used to make digging sticks, bows, handles and halibut hooks.

■**LOCAL SITES** Often seen as trailside thickets. Between Nitinat Narrows and the Cheewhat River is a tunnel that has been worn through the 5- to 7-m trees that line both sides of the boardwalk.

BITTER CHERRY
Prunus emarginata • Rose family: *Rosaceae*

■**DESCRIPTION** Bitter cherry is a small to medium-size tree, 5-15 m in height. Its bark is very distinctive: reddy brown with orange slits (lenticels), it is thin, smooth and peels horizontally. The white flowers (1 cm across) put on a wonderful show in April. The immature green fruit, 1 cm across, appear in early June and are bright red by midsummer. The leaves are quite different from those of the familiar Japanese cherries; they are alternate, 3-8 cm long, very finely toothed and usually rounded at the tip. The cherries are extremely bitter and considered inedible to humans, but are an important food source for birds. The fruit pits do not break down when digested, so birds carry them many kilometres from the parent tree.

■**HABITAT** Scattered in disturbed forests at low to mid elevations.

■**NATIVE USE** The shiny red bark was used to make baskets, mats and bags. The hard wood makes excellent fuel.

■**LOCAL SITES** Common in the Port Renfrew area; very noticeable when flowering in mid-April.

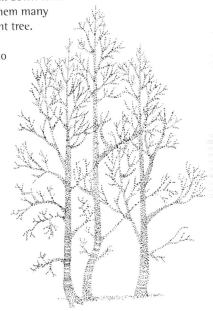

WILLOWS
Salix sp. • Willow family: *Salicaceae*

■**DESCRIPTION** Native willows are easy to identify as a genus but hard to distinguish as species. This is due to the variable leaf shapes within the same species, male and female flowers on separate plants, flowering before leaves appear and hybridization between species. The two most common willows are:

Scouler's willow (*Salix scouleriana*) — a shrub or tree 5-12 m in height, leaves 5-8 cm long, felty, narrow at the base and rounded at the tip. The flowers appear before the leaves, males to 4 cm long, females to 6 cm.

■**HABITAT** Scattered in disturbed spots in young forests at low to mid elevations.

Pacific willow (*Salix lucida* ssp. *lasiandra*) — a shrub or tree 6-12 m in height, leaves 10-15 cm long, lance-shaped, with finely toothed edges. The flower appears with the leaves, males to 7 cm long, females to 12 cm.

■**HABITAT** Commonly seen in shallow fresh water, ditches, creeks and at lakesides. Low to mid elevations.

Scouler's Willow

Pacific Willow

< *Pacific Willow*

Tsusiat Falls, the most spectacular falls on the trail

Cabin near Pachena Bay

PACIFIC SILVER FIR

Abies amabilis • Pine family: *Pinaceae*

■**DESCRIPTION** Pacific silver fir is a straight-trunked, symmetrical conifer to 60 m in height. The bark on young trees is smooth grey, with prominent vertical resin blisters. As the tree ages the bark becomes scaly, rougher and often lighter in colour. The cones are dark purple, barrel-shaped to 12 cm long, and sit erect on the upper portion of the tree. The needles are a lustrous dark green on the upper surface, silvery white below, with a notched tip. Pacific silver fir is one of Canada's stateliest conifers. The species name *amabilis* means "lovely fir."

■**HABITAT** Moist forests at mid to high elevations.

■**NATIVE USE** The soft wood was used for fuel, but little else. The sap was enjoyed as a chewing gum.

■**LOCAL SITES** Small groves of trees from 25 to 60 cm in diameter appear between Pachena Bay and Michigan Creek, with spotty sightings after that. The foliage starts very high; look for smooth grey bark with vertical blisters. The tallest Pacific silver fir in B.C. is 43.9 m.

YELLOW CYPRESS or YELLOW CEDAR

Chamaecyparis nootkatensis • Cypress family: *Cupressaceae*

■DESCRIPTION Yellow cypress is a large, slow-growing conifer of conical habit that often exceeds 45 m in height. Its thin, greyish brown bark can be shed in vertical strips. The reddish brown cones are round, to 1-2 cm across, with 4-6 scales tipped with pointed bosses (red cedar has egg-shaped cones). The bluish green leaves are prickly to touch and more pendulous than the red cedar's. Yellow cypress was first documented in Nootka Sound on the west coast of Vancouver Island in 1791 by Archibald Menzies, hence the species name. Its genus name is now being changed to *Cupressus*.

■HABITAT On the southern coast it grows in moist forests at mid to high elevations.

■NATIVE USE The wood was used for carving fine objects such as bentwood boxes, chests and intricately carved canoe paddles. The bark is softer than red cedar's and women used it to make clothing, blankets, baskets, rope and hats.

■LOCAL SITES Large single trees in the Bamfield area, more dominant at higher levels. The tallest yellow cypress in B.C. is 62 m.

< *The distinct pendulous profile of the yellow cypress, on the right in this photo (top)*

■**DESCRIPTION** Sitka spruce is often seen on rocky outcrops as a twisted dwarf tree, though in favourable conditions it can exceed 90 m in height. Its reddish brown bark is thin and patchy, a good identifier when the branches are too high to observe. The cones are gold brown, to 8 cm long. The needles are dark green, to 3 cm long and sharp to touch. Sitka spruce has the highest strength-to-weight ratio of any B.C. tree. It was used to build the frame of Howard Hughes' infamous plane *Spruce Goose*.

■**HABITAT** A temperate rainforest tree that does not grow farther than 200 km from the ocean.

■**NATIVE USE** The new shoots and inner bark were a good source of vitamin C. The best baskets and hats were woven from spruce roots, and the pitch (sap) was often chewed as a gum.

■**LOCAL SITES** Sitka spruce is the most common conifer on the trail. Gnarled, windswept miniatures can be seen hanging on cliff edges (for example, at Tsuquadra Point) and singular rock outcrops (Bonilla Point). There is an exceptional grove of first-growth trees over 2 m in diameter between the Klanawa River and Trestle Creek. The tallest Sitka spruce in the world, 95.8 m, is up Carmanah Creek on Vancouver Island.

Pinus contorta: var. *contorta* • Pine family: *Pinaceae*

■DESCRIPTION Depending on where they are growing, shore pines vary dramatically in size and shape. By the shoreline they are usually stunted and twisted from harsh winds and nutrient-deficient soil. A little farther inland they can be straight-trunked to 20 m in height. The small cones, 3-5 cm long, are often slightly lopsided and remain on the tree for many years. The dark green needles are 4-7 cm long and grow in bundles of two. The nuts are edible but small and hard to reach. Another variety, lodgepole pine (*P. contorta* var. *latifolia*), grows straighter and taller, to 40 m.

■HABITAT The coastal variety grows in the driest and wettest coastal sites, from low to high elevations.

■NATIVE USE The straight wood was used for teepee poles, torches and arrow and harpoon shafts.

■LOCAL SITES A wonderful assortment of stunted shore pines grows in the elevated bog between Logan Creek and Walbran Creek, and there is a grove of 4- to 9-m trees behind the lookout at the top of Valencia Bluffs.

DOUGLAS FIR

Pseudotsuga menziesii • Pine family: *Pinaceae*

■**DESCRIPTION** Douglas fir is a tall, fast-growing conifer to 90 m in height. Its bark is thick, corky and deeply furrowed. The ovate cones are 7-10 cm long and have 3 forked bracts protruding from the scales; the cones hang down from the branches, unlike true firs' cones, which stand up. The needles are 2-3 cm long, pointed at the apex, with a slight groove on the top and two white bands of stomata on the underside. The common name commemorates the botanist and explorer David Douglas.

111

■**HABITAT** Can tolerate dry to moist conditions from low to high elevations. Reaches its tallest size near the coast.

■**NATIVE USE** The wood was used for teepee poles, smoking racks, spear shafts, fishhooks and firewood.

■**LOCAL SITES** While Sitka spruce dominates most of the trail, Douglas fir grows farther inland, starting at the Nitinat Lake area. The tallest Douglas fir in Canada is 94.3 m.

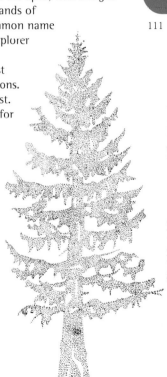

WESTERN RED CEDAR
Thuja plicata • Cypress family: *Cupressaceae*

■**DESCRIPTION** Western red cedar is a large, fast-growing conifer with heights exceeding 60 m. Its bark sheds vertically and ranges from cinnamon red on young trees to grey on mature ones. The bases of older trees are usually heavily flared, with deep furrows. The egg-shaped cones are 1 cm long, green when young, turning brown and upright when mature (yellow cypress has round cones). The bright green leaves are scale-like, with an overlapping-shingle appearance.

113

Western red cedar is B.C.'s provincial tree. On old stumps, springboard marks can be seen 2-3 m above the ground; these allowed early fallers to get away from the flared bases. The shingle industry is now the biggest user of red cedar.

■**HABITAT** Thrives on moist ground at low elevations. Will tolerate drier or higher sites but will not attain gigantic proportions.

■**NATIVE USE** First Nations people know this tree as "the tree of life." It supplied them from birth to death, from cradle to coffin. The wood was used to make dugout canoes, fishing floats, paddles, bowls, masks, totem poles, ornamental boxes and spear and arrow shafts. The bark was shredded for clothing, diapers, mats, blankets, baskets and medicine.

■**LOCAL SITES** At Red Creek, enormous cedars 4 m in diameter guard the Red Creek Fir. There are many 2-m-diameter trees between 150-Yard Creek and Camper Creek. The tallest western red cedar in B.C. is 59.2 m.

WESTERN HEMLOCK
Tsuga heterophylla • Pine family: *Pinaceae*

■DESCRIPTION Western hemlock is a fast-growing pyramidal conifer to 60 m in height. Its reddish brown bark becomes thick and deeply furrowed on mature trees. The plentiful cones are small (2-2.5 cm long), conical and reddish when young. The flat, light green leaves vary in size from 0.5 to 2 cm long. The main leaders and new shoots are nodding, giving the tree a soft, pendulous appearance that is good for identification. Western hemlock is the state tree of Washington.

■HABITAT Flourishes on the Pacific coast from Alaska to Oregon and from low levels to 1,000 m, where it is replaced by mountain hemlock (*T. mertensiana*).

■NATIVE USE The wood has long been used for spear shafts, spoons, dishes, roasting spits and ridgepoles. The bark was boiled to make a red dye for wool and basket material.

■LOCAL SITES Common on forested side of the trail. Large specimens can be seen between 150-Yard Creek and Camper Creek. The largest consistent grove is between Nitinat Narrows and Tsusiat Falls. An excellent collection of natural bonsai hemlock can be seen from the boardwalks through the elevated bogs between Cullite Creek and Walbran Creek; some of these miniatures are probably hundreds of years old. B.C.'s tallest hemlock, 75.6 m, is near Tahsish River on the west coast of Vancouver Island.

WESTERN WHITE PINE
Pinus monticola • Pine family: *Pinaceae*

■**DESCRIPTION** Western white pine is a medium-size symmetrical conifer to 40 m in height. Its bark is silver grey when young, dark brown and scaly when old. The cones are 15-25 cm long and slightly curved. The bluish green needles are 5-10 cm long and grow in bundles of 5. The species name *monticola* means "growing on mountains."

■**HABITAT** On the southern coast it grows on moist to wet soils at low to high elevations.

■**NATIVE USE** The bark was peeled in strips and sewn together with roots to make pine-bark canoes. The pitch was used for waterproofing.

■**LOCAL SITES** An extensive grove can be seen in the elevated bog between Cullite Creek and Logan Creek. The trees range in height from 1-m bonsais to 10-m specimens that are freely producing cones.

WESTERN YEW or PACIFIC YEW
Taxus brevifolia • Yew family: *Taxaceae*

■**DESCRIPTION** Western yew is a small conifer from 3 to 15 m in height. It is usually seen as a straggly shrub or small tree in the understory of larger trees. Its thin brownish bark is scale-like, exposing reddish purple patches that distinguish it from the European species. Female trees produce a beautiful but poisonous red berry that ripens in August/September. The flat needles are 2-3 cm long, dark green above with white bands below. The cancer-fighting drug Taxol is extracted from yew bark.

117

CAUTION: the berries are considered poisonous.

■**HABITAT** Found intermittently on moist forested sites at low to mid levels.

■**NATIVE USE** Western yew was considered the best wood for making bows.

■**LOCAL SITES** Smaller trees can be seen scattered alongside the trail, and larger ones in the Bamfield area. The tallest yew in B.C., 22.25 m, is at Fulford Harbour on Saltspring Island.

Achene	A small, dry, one-seeded fruit (e.g., sunflower seeds).
Anther	The pollen-bearing (top) portion of the stamen.
Axil	The angle made between a stalk and a stem on which it is growing.
Biennial	Completing its life cycle in two growing seasons.
Bloom	A fine, powdery covering on stems, leaves or fruit.
Boss	Knob-like studs, as in the points on cones of yellow cypress.
Bract	A modified leaf below the flower.
Catkin	A spike-like or drooping flower cluster, male or female (e.g., cottonwood).
Deciduous	A plant that sheds its leaves annually, usually in the autumn.
Dioecious	Male and female flowers on separate plants.
Epiphyte	A plant that grows on another plant for physical support, without robbing the host plant of nutrients.
Herbaceous perennial	A nonwoody plant that dies back to the ground each year and regrows the following season.
Lenticel	Raised organs that replace stomata on a stem.
Node	The place on a stem where the leaves and auxiliary buds are attached.
Obovate	Oval in shape, with the narrower end pointing downward, like an upside down egg.
Panicle	A branched inflorescence.
Petiole	The stalk of a leaf.
Pinnate	A compound leaf with the leaflets arranged on both sides of a central axis.
Pinnule	Leaflet of a pinnately compound leaf.
Rhizome	An underground modified stem. Runners and stolons are on top of the ground.

Scape	A leafless stem rising from the ground. It may support one or many flowers.
Sepal	The outer parts of a flower, usually green, collectively called the "calyx."
Sori	Spore cases.
Stipe	Stalk (petiole), usually referring to ferns.
Stolon	A stem or branch that runs along the surface of the ground and takes root at the nodes or apex, forming new plants.
Stomata	The pores in the epidermis of leaves, usually seen as white.
Style	The stem of the pistil (female organ).
Tepal	A term used when there is no distinction between the sepals and petals.

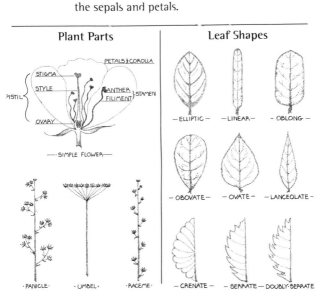

Plant Parts

PETALS & COROLLA
STIGMA
STYLE
PISTIL
ANTHER
FILIMENT } STAMEN
OVARY
—SIMPLE FLOWER—

· PANICLE ·   · UMBEL ·   · RACEME ·

Leaf Shapes

— ELLIPTIC —   — LINEAR —   — OBLONG —

— OBOVATE —   — OVATE —   — LANCEOLATE —

— CRENATE —   — SERRATE —   — DOUBLY-SERRATE —

Adolph, Val. *Tales of the Trees*. Key Books, Delta, B.C., 2000

Allen, George. *Timeless Shore, Canada's West Coast Trail*. Bayeux Arts Incorporated, Calgary, Alberta, 1994

Clark, Lewis J. *Wild Flowers of British Columbia*. Gray's Publishing Ltd., Sidney, B.C., 1973

Craighead, John J., Frank C. Craighead, Jr., and Ray J. Davis. *A Field Guide to Rocky Mountain Wildflowers*. Houghton Mifflin Company, Boston, Massachusetts, 1963

Haskin, L.L. *Wild Flowers of the Pacific Coast*. Binford and Mort, Portland, Oregon, 1934 (republished 1977, Dover Publications, New York)

Klinka, K., V. J. Krajina, A. Ceska and A. M. Scagel. *Indicator Plants of Coastal British Columbia*. University of British Columbia Press, Vancouver, B.C., 1989

Lyons, C. P. *Trees, Shrubs and Flowers to Know in British Columbia*. J. M. Dent and Sons, Toronto, Ontario and Vancouver, B.C., 1976 (1st ed. 1952)

Pojar, Jim and MacKinnon, Andy. *Plants of the Pacific Northwest Coast*. Lone Pine Publishing, Vancouver, B.C. 1994

Sargent, Charles Sprague. *Manual of the Trees of North America*. Dover Publications, New York, 1965, two volumes (originally published in 1905 by Houghton Mifflin Company, Boston, Massachusetts)

Sierra Club of Western Canada. *The West Coast Trail and Nitinat Lakes*. Douglas and McIntyre, Vancouver, B.C., 1987

Stoltmann, Randy. *Hiking Guide to the Big Trees of Southwestern British Columbia*. Western Canada Wilderness Committee, Vancouver, B.C., 1987

Szczawinski, A. F., and George A. Hardy. *Guide to Common Edible Plants of British Columbia*. Handbook No. 20, Royal British Columbia Museum, Victoria, B.C., 1974

Turner, Nancy J. *Plants in British Columbia Indian Technology*. Handbook No. 38, Royal British Columbia Museum, Victoria, B.C., 1979